Rookie
Read-About® Health

Exercise

By Sharon Gordon

Consultants

Nanci Vargus, Ed.D.
Primary Multiage Teacher
Decatur Township Schools, Indianapolis, Indiana

Jayne L. Waddell, R.N., M.A., L.P.C.
School Nurse/Health Educator/Lic. Professional Counselor

Children's Press®
A Division of Scholastic Inc.
New York   Toronto   London   Auckland   Sydney
Mexico City   New Delhi   Hong Kong
Danbury, Connecticut

Designer: Herman Adler Design
Photo Researcher: Caroline Anderson
The photo on the cover shows children running.

Library of Congress Cataloging-in-Publication Data

Gordon, Sharon.
  Exercise / by Sharon Gordon.
    p. cm. — (Rookie read-about health)
  Includes index.
  Summary: Discusses the importance of exercise and describes different ways
to keep physically fit.
    ISBN 0-516-22571-5 (lib. bdg.)   0-516-26950-X (pbk.)
    1. Exercise—Juvenile literature. 2. Physical fitness—Juvenile literature.
[1. Exercise.] I. Title. II. Series.
  RA781 .G67 2002
  613.7′1—dc21

                                    2002005484

CHILDREN'S PRESS, AND ROOKIE READ-ABOUT®,
and associated logos are trademarks and or registered trademarks
of Grolier Publishing Co., Inc. SCHOLASTIC and associated logos
are trademarks and or registered trademarks of Scholastic Inc.

1 2 3 4 5 6 7 8 9 10 R 11 10 09 08 07 06 05 04 03 02

Try to touch your toes.
Can you do it?

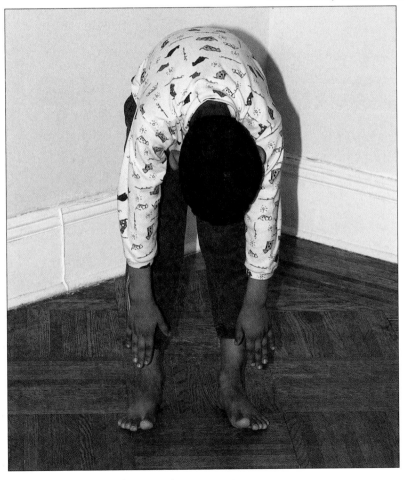

3

Exercise is good for your body. When you exercise, you move your body to stay fit.

Just like a car, your body
needs to be used.

A car that is not used does not work very well. The same is true for you!

Exercise helps your body stay strong. It helps you stay healthy.

You will even sleep better
at night.

Exercise helps you use all of your muscles. You have muscles from head to toe.

You could not push or pull without your muscles. You could not walk or run.

11

The more you use a muscle, the stronger it gets. How strong are your muscles?

Your heart is a very important muscle! Exercise helps to keep your heart strong.

You can exercise at home or in school. Playing outside with your friends is a good way to exercise.

15

Go slow when you first start to exercise. Do not do too much too fast. That could hurt your muscles, not help them.

You can get your exercise
in many different ways.
Try to find things you like
to do.

Do you like to play sports?
Go for it!

19

Some people take
dance lessons.

Others exercise in a karate class. What a workout!

So don't just sit there—
do something!

Take the dog for a walk.

Turn on some music
and dance!

Jump rope.
Shoot some hoops.

Splash in the water.

Do you like to run?
You can run in a race.

It's fun to exercise!

Words You Know

dance

exercise

healthy

jump rope

30

karate

run

strong

walk

31

Index

About the Author

Sharon Gordon is a writer living in Midland Park, New Jersey. She and her husband have three school-aged children and a spoiled pooch. Together they enjoy visiting the Outer Banks of North Carolina as often as possible.

Photo Credits

Photographs © 2002: Corbis Images/Kevin R. Morris: 11; Peter Arnold Inc./BIOS/Klein/Hubert: 23, 31 bottom right; Photo Researchers, NY: 25 (Ken Cavanagh), 21, 31 top left (Doug Martin); PhotoEdit: 29 (Rudi Von Briel), 5, 7, 30 top right (Mary Kate Denny), 8, 30 bottom left (Myrleen Ferguson Cate), 19 (Tony Freeman), 12, 31 bottom left (Robert Ginn), 15, 30 bottom right (R. Hutchings), 6 (John Neubauer), 26, 31 top right (Michael Newman), 16 (David Young-Wolff); Rigoberto Quinteros: 3; Superstock, Inc.: 9, 20, 30 top left; The Image Works/Bob Daemmrich: cover; Visuals Unlimited/Arthur R. Hill: 24.